ESSENTIAL TECHNIQUE
FOR BAND

INTERMEDIATE TO ADVANCED STUDIES

TIM LAUTZENHEISER

JOHN HIGGINS

CHARLES MENGHINI

PAUL LAVENDER

TOM C. RHODES

DON BIERSCHENK

To create an account, visit:
www.essentialelementsinteractive.com

Student Activation Code
E3BS-1475-9806-4831

ISBN 978-0-634-04416-8

HAL•LEONARD®
CORPORATION
7777 W. BLUEMOUND RD. P.O. BOX 13819 MILWAUKEE, WI 53213

G MAJOR (Concert B♭ Major)

1. SCALE AND ARPEGGIO

2. EXERCISE IN THIRDS

3. ARPEGGIO STUDY

4. TWO-PART ETUDE

5. CHROMATIC SCALE

6. BALANCE BUILDER

THEORY

divisi or *div.*	Divide the written parts among players, usually into two parts, with equal numbers playing each part.
unison or *a2*	All players play the same part (usually found after a divisi section).

7. CHORALE

*Remember to use Alternate F♯ (G♭) whenever F♯ follows or precedes F♮.

8. GREAT GATE OF KIEV

Modeste Mussorgsky

Maestoso ◁ *Bold, stately*

9. CHILDREN'S SHOES

Black American Spiritual

Allegro

English composer **George Frideric Handel** (1685–1759) is among the best known composers of the **Baroque Period (1600–1750)**. *Sound an Alarm* (from *Judas Maccabaeus*) and his most famous work, the *Hallelujah Chorus,* (from *Messiah*) are two well-known melodies from his **oratorios**, large scale works for solo voices, chorus, and orchestra.

HISTORY

10. SOUND AN ALARM

George Frideric Handel

C♯/D♭

Allegro

11. HALLELUJAH CHORUS

George Frideric Handel

Allegro

12. RHYTHM RAP *Clap the rhythm while counting and tapping.*

THEORY

$\frac{3}{8}$ **Time Signature** $\frac{3}{8}$ = **3 beats** per measure
= **Eighth** note gets one beat

♪ = 1 beat   ♩ = 2 beats   ♩. = 3 beats

3/8 time is usually played with a slight emphasis on the 1st beat of each measure. In faster music, this primary beat will make the music feel like it's counted "in 1."

13. RHYTHM RAP *Compare this exercise with No. 12.*

14. WALTZ PETITE

15. MOLLY BANN

English Folksong

THEORY

$\frac{9}{8}$ **Time Signature** $\frac{9}{8}$ = **9 beats** per measure
= **Eighth** note gets one beat

♪ = 1 beat   ♩. = 3 beats
♩ = 2 beats   ♩. = 6 beats

9/8 time is usually played with a slight emphasis on the **1st**, **4th**, and **7th** beats of each measure. This divides the measure into 3 groups of 3 beats each. In faster music, these three primary beats will make the music feel like it's counted "in 3."

16. RHYTHM RAP *Clap the rhythm while counting and tapping.*

17. SUNDAY AT NINE

E MINOR (Concert G Minor)

THEORY

Minor Keys

Minor keys and their scales sound different from major keys because of their different pattern of whole and half steps. Each minor key is *relative* or "related" to the major key with the same key signature.

The simplest form of a minor key is called **natural minor**. Two other types are **harmonic minor** and **melodic minor**, each of which have certain altered tones.

18. NATURAL MINOR *Practice both upper and lower octaves.*

19. HARMONIC MINOR

20. PAT-A-PAN

French

21. THE SLEDGEHAMMER SONG

Russian

22. ESSENTIAL ELEMENTS QUIZ – AUSTRALIAN FOLK SONG

Australian

C MAJOR (Concert E♭ Major)

23. SCALE AND ARPEGGIO *Practice both upper and lower octaves.*

24. EXERCISE IN THIRDS

B

25. ARPEGGIO STUDY

26. TWO-PART ETUDE

27. CHROMATIC SCALE

28. BALANCE BUILDER

29. CHORALE

Austrian composer **Johann Strauss Jr.** (1825–1899) is also known as "The Waltz King." He wrote some of the world's most famous waltzes (dances in 3/4 meter). This waltz is from *Die Fledermaus* ("The Bat"), Strauss' most famous **operetta**. Operettas were the forerunners of today's musicals, such as *Oklahoma, The Sound Of Music,* and *The Phantom Of The Opera*.

35. JACK'S THE MAN

12/8 Time Signature

12 = **12 beats** per measure
8 = **Eighth** note gets one beat

♪ = 1 beat   ♩. = 3 beats   ♩. ♩. = 9 beats
♩ = 2 beats   ♩. = 6 beats   𝅝. = 12 beats

12/8 time is usually played with a slight emphasis on the **1st**, **4th**, **7th** and **10th** beats of each measure. This divides the measure into 4 groups of 3 beats each. These four primary beats will make the music feel like it's counted "in 4."

36. RHYTHM RAP   *Clap the rhythm while counting and tapping.*

37. SERENADE

38. WITH THINE EYES

molto rit.
△ *molto* = "much"

A MINOR (Concert C Minor)

39. NATURAL MINOR

40. HARMONIC MINOR

Even today, **Native American Indian music** continues to be an important part of tribal dancing ceremonies, using Apache fiddles, rattles, flutes, and log drums to accompany simple songs. American composer **Charles Wakefield Cadman** (1881–1946) wrote this song in 1914 based on Indian melodies he researched throughout his lifetime.

HISTORY

41. SONG OF THE WEEPING SPIRIT

Native American Indian Melody
Adapt. Charles Wakefield Cadman

Lento mysterioso ◁ *Slowly and mysteriously*

42. SCOTTISH LEGEND

Amy Marcy Beach

43. ESSENTIAL ELEMENTS QUIZ *Which measures sound major and which ones minor?*

Andante

D MAJOR (Concert F Major)

44. SCALE AND ARPEGGIO *Practice both upper and lower octaves.*

45. EXERCISE IN THIRDS

46. ARPEGGIO STUDY

47. TWO-PART ETUDE

48. CHROMATIC SCALE

△ D♭ (C♯ *enharmonic*)

49. BALANCE BUILDER

50. CHORALE

51. REST ALERT

52. RHYTHM RAP

53. ISLAND SONG

French composer **Claude Debussy** (1862–1918) created moods and "impressions" with his music. While earlier composers used music to describe events (such as Tchaikovsky's *1812 Overture)*, Debussy's new ideas helped shape today's music. The style of art and music created in this time is called "impressionism." The first automobile was produced during Debussy's lifetime. He died the same year that World War I ended.

54. THE LITTLE CHILD

Claude Debussy

Triplets with Rests — Triplets that start or end with a rest are usually marked with a bracket

55. TRIPLET AND REST VARIATIONS

56. TURKEY IN THE STRAW

Allegretto

American Folk Song

57. ESSENTIAL ELEMENTS QUIZ *Write the first 2 lines of exercise 56 in cut time.*

THEORY

Sixteenth Notes and Rests
in $\frac{6}{8}$, $\frac{3}{8}$, $\frac{9}{8}$, $\frac{12}{8}$

♪ = ½ beat   𝄾 = ½ beat   ♩ = 2 beats   𝄽 = 2 beats
♩ = 1 beat   𝄾 = 1 beat   ♩. = 3 beats   𝄽· = 3 beats

58. RHYTHM RAP

59. SONATINA

B MINOR (Concert D Minor)

60. NATURAL MINOR *Practice both upper and lower octaves.*

61. HARMONIC MINOR

62. COSSACK MARCH

63. SLAVONIC DANCE NO. 2

Antonin Dvořák

64. ESSENTIAL ELEMENTS QUIZ – THE PRETTY GIRL

Irish

F MAJOR (Concert A♭ Major)

65. SCALE AND ARPEGGIO *Practice both upper and lower octaves.*

66. EXERCISE IN THIRDS

67. ARPEGGIO STUDY

Alternate fingering

68. TWO-PART ETUDE

69. CHROMATIC SCALE

70. BALANCE BUILDER

71. CHORALE

Andante

mf

rit.

The Star Spangled Banner is the national anthem of the United States of America. Francis Scott Key wrote the words during the 1814 battle at Fort McHenry. He listened to the sounds of the fighting throughout the night while being detained on a ship. At dawn, he saw the American flag still flying over the fort. He was inspired to write these words, which were later set to the melody of a popular English song.

72. THE STAR SPANGLED BANNER

Words by Francis Scott Key
Music by John Stafford Smith

Dynamics

pp – *pianissimo* (play very softly)   *ff* – *fortissimo* (play very loudly)
Remember to use full breath support to produce the best possible tone and intonation.

73. INTERMEZZO

74. RHYTHM RAP

75. MORNING STAR

Moderato

76. SONATA

Wolfgang Amadeus Mozart

Andante grazioso ◁ *Gracefully*

77. RONDEAU

Jean-Joseph Mouret

Allegro

THEORY

Grace Note ♪ A small note (or notes) which is played on, or slightly before the beat.

78. JULIET'S WALTZ

Charles Gounod

Tempo di valse

D MINOR (Concert F Minor)

79. NATURAL MINOR *Practice both upper and lower octaves.*

80. HARMONIC MINOR

81. SORCERER'S APPRENTICE

Paul Dukas

82. I WALK THE ROAD AGAIN

American

83. ESSENTIAL ELEMENTS QUIZ – GREENSLEEVES

English Folk Song

A MAJOR (Concert C Major)

84. SCALE AND ARPEGGIO

85. EXERCISE IN THIRDS

86. ARPEGGIO STUDY

E

Alternate fingering

87. TWO-PART ETUDE

A

B

88. CHROMATIC SCALE

89. BALANCE BUILDER

A

B

C

90. CHORALE

Andante

mf

rit.

Black American spirituals originated in the 1700's. As one of the largest categories of true American folk music, these melodies were sung and passed on for generations without being written down. Black and white people worked together to publish the first spiritual collection in 1867, four years after *The Emancipation Proclamation* was signed into law.

91. SIT DOWN, SISTER

Black American Spiritual

92. SPINNING SONG – Duet

Johann Ellmenreich

THEORY

Quarter Note Triplets

Similar to eighth note triplets where 1 beat is divided into 3 equal notes, quarter note triplets divide 2 beats into 3 equal notes.

93. RHYTHM RAP

▽ *1 beat divided into 3 notes.*

▽ *2 beats divided into 3 notes.*

Clap

1 2 3 4 1 2 trip - let 3 4 1 2 3 4 1 trip - let 3 4
                                                        (2)

94. THREE FOR TWO

95. SURIRAM'S SONG

Malaysian Folk Song

Allegro

mf

f *mf*

HISTORY

Africa is a large continent that is made up of many nations, and **African folk music** is as diverse as its many cultures. Folk songs from any country are expressions of work, love, war, sadness and joy. This song is from Tanzania. The words describe a rabbit hopping and running through a field. Listen to the percussion section play African-sounding drums and rhythms.

96. JIBULI (The Rabbit's Song)

Adapted Tanzanian Folk Song

Allegro

mf

p

mf *f*

F♯ MINOR (Concert A Minor)

97. NATURAL MINOR

98. HARMONIC MINOR

△ E♯ (F♮ enharmonic)

Meter Changes

THEORY

Meter changes, or changing time signatures within a section of music, are commonly found in contemporary music. Composers use this technique to create a unique rhythm, pulse, or musical style.

99. TIME ZONES

HISTORY

Important French composers of the late 19th century include **Claude Debussy** (1862–1918), **Gabriel Fauré** (1845–1924), **Erik Satie** (1866–1925), **César Franck** (1822–1890), **Camille Saint-Saëns** (1835–1921), and **Paul Dukas** (1865–1935). Their works continue to have influence on the music of modern day composers. Gabriel Fauré wrote *Pavanne* (originally for orchestra) in 1887, two years before the Eiffel Tower was completed in Paris.

100. PAVANNE

Gabriel Fauré

Bb MAJOR (Concert Db Major)

101. SCALE AND ARPEGGIO *Practice both upper and lower octaves.*

102. EXERCISE IN THIRDS

103. ARPEGGIO STUDY

104. TWO-PART ETUDE

105. CHROMATIC SCALE

106. BALANCE BUILDER

107. CHORALE

*Forked Bb (F) is convenient to use when playing a Bb major arpeggio.

24

112. SUKURU ITO

Moderato

African Folk Song

mf

HISTORY

English composer **George Frideric Handel** (1685–1759) lived during the **Baroque Period (1600–1750)**. *Water Music* was written in honor of England's King George I. The first performance took place on the Thames River on July 17, 1717. Fifty musicians performed the work while floating on a barge. Handel lived during the same time as Johann Sebastian Bach, perhaps the most famous Baroque composer.

113. WATER MUSIC

Allegro maestoso

George Frideric Handel

f

114. ESSENTIAL TECHNIQUE QUIZ – PICTURES AT AN EXHIBITION

Maestoso

Modeste Mussorgsky

f

G MINOR (Concert B♭ Minor)

115. NATURAL MINOR

116. HARMONIC MINOR

Ostinato A clear and distinct musical phrase that is repeated persistently.

British composer **Gustav Holst** (1874–1934) is one of the most widely played composers for concert band today. Many of his compositions, including his familiar military suites, are based on tuneful English folk songs. His most famous work for orchestra, *The Planets (1916),* has seven movements—one written for each known planet, excluding Earth. At this time, Pluto was undiscovered.

117. MARS – Duet/Trio

Gustav Holst

E MAJOR (Concert G Major)

118. SCALE AND ARPEGGIO *Practice both upper and lower octaves.*

119. EXERCISE IN THIRDS

120. ARPEGGIO STUDY

121. TWO-PART ETUDE

122. CHROMATIC SCALE

123. BALANCE BUILDER

124. CHORALE

Norwegian composer **Edvard Grieg** (1843–1907) based much of his music on the folk songs and dances of Norway. During the late 19th century, composers often used melodies from their native land. This trend is called **nationalism**. Russian **Modeste Mussorgsky** (1839–1881), Czech **Antonin Dvořák** (1841–1904), and Englishman **Sir Edward Elgar** (1857–1934) are other famous composers whose music was influenced by nationalism.

125. NORWEGIAN DANCE

Edvard Grieg

126. FRENCH NATIONAL ANTHEM (LA MARSEILLAISE)

Rouget De L'Isle

Music written during the **Renaissance Period (1430–1600)** was often upbeat and dance-like. *Wolsey's Wilde* was originally written for the lute, an ancestor to the guitar and the most popular instrument of the Renaissance era. Modern day concert band composer Gordon Jacob used this popular song in his *William Byrd Suite,* written as a tribute to English composer William Byrd (1543–1623).

127. WOLSEY'S WILDE

Anonymous

C# MINOR (Concert E Minor)

128. NATURAL MINOR *Practice both upper and lower octaves.*

129. HARMONIC MINOR

B# (C♮ *enharmonic*)

HISTORY

Native Japanese instruments include the *shakuhachi*, a bamboo flute played pointing downward; the *koto*, a long zither with movable frets played sitting down; and the *gakubiwa*, a pear-shaped lute with strings that are plucked. These instruments have been an important part of Japanese culture since the 8th century. *Kabuki*, a Japanese theatrical form that originated in 1603, remains popular in Japan. Performers play native Japanese instruments during Kabuki performances.

130. SONG OF THE SHAKUHACHI

Japanese Folk Song

THEORY

D.C. al Coda At the **D.C. al Coda**, play again from the beginning to the indication **To Coda** ⊕, then skip to the section marked ⊕ **Coda**, meaning "ending section."

D.S. al Coda Similar to **D.C. al Coda**, but return to the sign 𝄋.

131. POLOVETZIAN DANCES

Alexander Borodin

29

B MAJOR (Concert D Major)

132. SCALE AND ARPEGGIO *Practice both upper and lower octaves.*

133. EXERCISE IN THIRDS

134. ARPEGGIO STUDY

135. TWO-PART ETUDE

136. CHORALE

G# MINOR (Concert B Minor)

137. NATURAL MINOR

138. HARMONIC MINOR

F✕ (F double sharp) – enharmonic to G♮

Latin American Music combines the folk music from South and Central America, the Carribean Islands, American Indian, Spanish, and Portuguese cultures. Melodies are often accompanied by drums, maracas, and claves. Latin American music continues to influence jazz, classical, and popular styles of music. *Cielito Lindo* is a Latin American love song.

139. CIELITO LINDO

C. Fernandez

Tchaikovsky, along with Wagner, Brahms, Mendelssohn, and Chopin, helped define the musical era known as the **Romantic Period (1825–1900)**. The "symphonic tone poem" from this period continues to be one of the most popular musical forms performed by orchestras and bands today.

140. WALTZ IN FIVE (from SYMPHONY NO. 6)

Peter I. Tchaikovsky

141. THE YOUNG CHEVALIER

Scottish

*Alternate fingering "Bis" for B♭ (A♯) is commonly used, but *never* in chromatic passages.

E♭ MAJOR (Concert G♭ Major)

142. SCALE AND ARPEGGIO *Practice both upper and lower octaves.*

143. EXERCISE IN THIRDS

144. ARPEGGIO STUDY

145. TWO-PART ETUDE

146. CHORALE

C MINOR (Concert E♭ Minor)

147. NATURAL MINOR

148. HARMONIC MINOR

INDIVIDUAL STUDY – Baritone Saxophone

149. STUDY IN CONCERT C MAJOR

INDIVIDUAL STUDY – Baritone Saxophone

154. ARTICULATION STUDY

CD Track 7

155. 16TH NOTE PATTERNS AND ARTICULATION *Try using Bis fingering for B♭'s.*

CD Track 8

156. CONCERT F MINOR EXERCISE

CD Track 9

157. TRIPLET WORKOUT

CD Track 10

READING SKILL BUILDERS

158. READING SKILL BUILDER NO. 1

CD Track 11

159. READING SKILL BUILDER NO. 2

CD Track 12

160. READING SKILL BUILDER NO. 3

CD Track 13

161. READING SKILL BUILDER NO. 4

CD Track 14

162. READING SKILL BUILDER NO. 5

CD Track 15

REA--ING SKILL BUIL--ERS

163. READING SKILL BUILDER NO. 6

CD Track 16

164. READING SKILL BUILDER NO. 7

CD Track 17

165. READING SKILL BUILDER NO. 8

CD Track 18

166. READING SKILL BUILDER NO. 9

CD Track 19

167. CHORALE (Prelude from Hansel and Gretel) *CD Track 20*

Engelbert Humperdinck
Arr. by John Higgins

168. CHORALE (Based on a Theme by Palestrina) *CD Track 21*

Arr. by John Higgins

169. CHORALE (Based on a Theme by J. S. Bach) *CD Track 22*

Arr. by John Higgins

170. CHORALE (Based on a Theme by Tchaikovsky) *CD Track 23*

Arr. by John Higgins

171. CHORALE (Erhalt Uns In Der Wahrheit) *CD Track 24*

Johann Sebastian Bach
Arr. by John Higgins

172. CHORALE (Navy Hymn) *CD Track 25*

John Dykes
Arr. by John Higgins

173. CHORALE (Prelude) *CD Track 26*

Frederic Chopin
Arr. by John Higgins

RHYTHM STUDIES

RHYTHM STUDIES

THE BASICS OF JAZZ STYLE

from Essential Elements for Jazz Ensemble

Accenting "2 and 4"

For most traditional music the important beats in 4/4 time are 1 and 3. In jazz, however, the emphasis is usually on beats 2 and 4. Emphasizing "2 and 4" gives the music a jazz feeling.

Traditional   Jazz

174. ACCENTING 2 AND 4 *CD Track 47*

Jazz Articulations

These are the four basic articulations in jazz.

Tenuto
(full value)

Staccato
(short, unaccented)

Long Accent
(full value, accented)

Roof Top Accent
(short, accented)

Swing 8th Notes Sound Different Than They Look

In swing, the 2nd 8th note of each beat is actually played like the last third of a triplet, and slightly accented. 8th notes in swing style are usually played legato.

175. SWING 8TH NOTES *CD Track 48*

Quarter Notes

Quarter notes in swing style are usually played detached (staccato) with accents on beats 2 and 4.

176. QUARTERS AND 8THS *CD Track 49*

177. RUNNIN' AROUND *CD Track 50*

Syncopation in Jazz

When beats are played early (anticipated) or played late (delayed), the music becomes syncopated. Syncopation makes the music sound "jazzy."

178. WHEN THE SAINTS GO MARCHING IN – Without Syncopation *CD Track 51*

James Black and Katherine Purvis

179. WHEN THE SAINTS GO MARCHING IN – With Syncopation *CD Track 52*

"Jazzin' Up" the Melody by Adding Rhythms

Adding rhythms to a melody is another easy way to improvise in a jazz style. Start by filling out long notes with repeated 8th and quarter notes. Remember to swing the 8th notes (play legato and give the upbeats an accent).

180. "JAZZIN' UP" JINGLE BELLS *CD Track 53*

J. Pierpont

MAKE UP YOUR OWN (IMPROVISE) *CD Track 54*

181. LONDON BRIDGE

Complete the melody in your own "jazzed up" way. Use only the notes shown in parentheses. Slashes on the staff indicate when to improvise.

THEORY

Major Scales

Play major scales as part of your daily practice routine. Play all octaves, keys, and arpeggios, at various dynamic levels and tempos. Keep a steady pulse. Try different articulation patterns, such as:

182. G MAJOR (Concert B♭ Major) *CD Track 55*

183. C MAJOR (Concert E♭ Major) *CD Track 56*

184. D MAJOR (Concert F Major) *CD Track 57*

185. A MAJOR (Concert C Major) *CD Track 58*

186. F MAJOR (Concert A♭ Major) *CD Track 59*

187. Bb MAJOR (Concert Db Major) *CD Track 60*

188. E MAJOR (Concert G Major) *CD Track 61*

189. B MAJOR (Concert D Major) *CD Track 62*

190. F# MAJOR (Concert A Major) *CD Track 63*

191. Eb MAJOR (Concert Gb Major) *CD Track 64*

44

THEORY

Minor Scales

Play minor scales as part of your daily practice routine. Play all octaves, all three forms and the arpeggios at various dynamic levels and tempos. Keep a steady pulse. Try different articulation patterns, such as:

A.   B.   C.

192. B MINOR SCALE (Concert D Minor)

193. E MINOR SCALE (Concert G Minor)

194. A MINOR SCALE (Concert C Minor)

195. D MINOR SCALE (Concert F Minor)

TRILL CHART

Here are some common trill fingerings.

FINGERING CHART

E♭ BARITONE SAXOPHONE

Instrument Care Reminders

Before putting your instrument back in its case after playing, do the following:

- Remove the reed, wipe off excess moisture and return it to the reed case.
- Remove the mouthpiece and wipe the inside with a clean cloth. Once a week, wash the mouthpiece with warm tap water. Dry thoroughly.
- Loosen the neck screw and remove the neck. Shake out excess moisture and dry the neck with a neck cleaner.
- Use a body swab to dry the inside of your instrument. Or, drop the weight of a chamois or cotton swab into the bell. Pull the swab through the body several times. Return the instrument to its case.
- Your case is designed to hold only specific objects. If you try to force anything else into the case, it may damage your instrument.

○ = Open
● = Pressed down

The most common fingering appears first when two fingerings are shown.

Instrument courtesy of Yamaha Corporation of America, Band and Orchestral Division

FINGERING CHART

E♭ BARITONE SAXOPHONE

G♯ A♭

A

A♯ B♭ — "side" "forked" "bis"

B

C

C♯ D♭

D

D♯ E♭

E

F

F♯ G♭ — Alt.

G

G♯ A♭

A

A♯ B♭ — "side" "forked" "bis"

B

C

C♯ D♭

D

D♯ E♭

E — Alt.

F — Alt.

REFERENCE INDEX

Definitions (pg.)

Allegro Agitato   17
Allegro Marziale   27
Allegro Vivo   13
Andante Espressivo   23
Andante Grazioso   16
Animato   27
D.C. al Coda   28
D.S. al Coda   28
Divisi (*div.*)   2
Energetico   25
5/4   23
Fortissimo (*ff*)   15
Giocoso   11
Grace Note   16
Lento   8
Lento Mysterioso   9
Maestoso   3
Meter Changes   21
Minor Keys   5
Molto Rit.   8
9/8   4
Ostinato   25
Quarter Note Triplets   20
Pianissimo (*pp*)   15
16th Notes and Rests
   in 6/8, 3/8, 9/8, 12/8   12
Tempo Di Valse   7
3/8   4
Triplets with Rests   11
12/8   8
Unison (*a2*)   2

Composers

JOHANN SEBASTIAN BACH
• Joy   23

ALEXANDER BORODIN
• Polovetzian Dances   28

CLAUDE DEBUSSY
• The Little Child   11

PAUL DUKAS
• Sorcerer's Apprentice   17

ANTONIN DVORÁK
• Slavonic Dance No. 2   13

JOHANN ELLMENREICH
• Spinning Song   19

GABRIEL FAURÉ
• Pavanne   21

CHARLES GOUNOD
• Juliet's Waltz   16

EDVARD GRIEG
• Norwegian Dance   27

GEORGE FRIDERIC HANDEL
• Hallelujah Chorus   3
• Sound An Alarm   3
• Water Music   24

FRANZ JOSEF HAYDN
• German National Anthem   23

GUSTAV HOLST
• Mars   25

JEAN-JOSEPH MOURET
• Rondeau   16

WOLFGANG AMADEUS MOZART
• Sonata   16

MODESTE MUSSORGSKY
• Great Gate of Kiev   3
• Pictures at an Exhibition   24

JOHANN STRAUSS JR.
• Adele's Song   7

PETER I. TCHAIKOVSKY
• Waltz in Five
   (from Symphony No. 6)   30

World Music

AFRICAN
• Jibuli   20
• Sukuru Ito   24

AMERICAN
• Children's Shoes   3
• I Walk the Road Again   17
• The Keel Row   7
• Keepin' Secrets   7
• Sit Down, Sister   19
• Star Spangled Banner   15
• Turkey in the Straw   12

AUSTRALIAN
• Australian Folk Song   5

ENGLISH
• Greensleeves   17
• Molly Bann   4
• Wolsey's Wilde   27

FRENCH
• Pat-A-Pan   5
• French National Anthem   27

IRISH
• The Pretty Girl   13

JAPANESE
• Song of the Shakuhachi   28

LATIN AMERICAN
• Cielito Lindo   30

MALAYSIAN
• Suriram's Song   20

NATIVE AMERICAN INDIAN
• Song of the Weeping Spirit   9

RUSSIAN
• The Sledgehammer Song   5

SCOTTISH
• Scottish Legend   9
• The Young Chevalier   30